D1029023

IN 1887

The Immigrant in 1887

by JOHN W. NORDSTROM

First printed at the Dogwood Press, 1950
with sketches by Phyllis Heady

Eighth printing, April 2013
Printed in Canada

I AM WRITING THIS FOR MY GRANDCHILDREN to read after I am gone, to let them know what the average immigrant had to go through in the 1880s. Not that it was any worse for me than a lot of others, but after reading this they should be very happy that they were born in America.

I was born in Alvik Neder Lulea, Sweden, February 15, 1871. My father and mother had a small farm in this northernmost part of Sweden, where there were long, cold winters and very nice summers. My father passed away when I was eight years old, leaving my mother, a brother eighteen, a sister fourteen, a sister six and a brother three months old. My father had been a blacksmith and a wagon maker, and earned money on the side by having the farm, so his family got along very nicely.

My brother had learned the trade from our father so, after his death, continued at the trade with the assistance of a hired man on the farm. This continued for about three years and I was then eleven years old. By that time my family thought that I had had enough schooling and took me out of school to do the work of the hired man.

I got along well with a little help from my older brother and for four years I was very happy at home. When I was fifteen my brother got married and brought his young wife to our home, where we all lived together for that first winter. That is when the trouble started. My mother and my sister-in-law did not get along at all, quarreling all the time, till I got so sick of hearing them that I would go out to the barn and stay with the horses so I would not have to listen to them. I am sure that they were both at fault.

So then, according to my father's will, my brother was to have half of the farm and my mother and I the other half. My brother and I were to pay our sisters their share in money. The baby brother died when he was a year old. My older brother received the half of the farm on which were located the barn, house and other farm buildings, making it necessary for Mother and me to build a house and barn on our share of the property. I had to haul logs from the woods, about six miles away, after which Mother hired men to build the buildings. The houses those days were all built of logs because of the bitter cold winters.

By this time my mother seemed to think I was a man, and often remarked that at my age my brother could do nearly anything and why couldn't I. I often cried when I had trouble doing things she expected me to do and couldn't, and felt very helpless.

The winter I was sixteen years old I was so unhappy that I wanted to leave home. My reason for mentioning this is that so many people have asked me how I came to leave home so young. When I first asked my mother if I could go to America, she did not object but said I would have to rustle my own money for the fare.

As I knew that there was a little money left me by my father, I went to see our guardian and asked him if I could have the money for my fare to America. He had no right to let me have it before I was twenty-one years old, but gave his consent. I received four hundred and fifty crowns or about one hundred and twelve dollars. With it I bought a suit of clothes, the first clothes I had ever had on my back that were not homespun and hand woven. I might add here that I always thought the reason my mother was not against my going was that she intended to marry again, and I was not wrong, for she did marry again two years after I left home.

In those years there were no railroads in the northern part of Sweden. I must mention here that there were two young men twenty years old taking the trip with me. We took a two-day boat trip to Stockholm, went by canal boat across Sweden through the Gota Canal, which took about three days, to Gothenburg. From there we got on a boat to Hull, England, then took a train to Liverpool, England. That was the first time any of us had ever been on a train.

From Liverpool we got steerage passage to New York, which took ten days. The food was very bad and we were all seasick most of the time. On arriving at New York we landed at Castle Garden and immediately took a train to Stambaugh, Michigan, getting there on the third day we had been in America, each with only five dollars apiece left in our pockets.

When we reached Stambaugh all we could see was the little red depot in a gulch, and, as the station master could not understand us, we didn't know what to do. We stayed around there about two hours until a young man came along. He could easily see that we were greenhorns and came over and spoke Swedish to us. This made us very happy and he asked us if we knew anyone in Stambaugh. We said we had the name and address of a cousin of mine, Samuel Berlin, and he said my that was funny, for Mr. Berlin was his room partner. They were both bartenders but not on the same shift.

He took us up the road and up a hill and when we got to the top of the hill there was the town in a valley on the other side. It was a village of five or six hundred people, three saloons, two or three stores and some boarding houses for the miners who worked in the iron mines close by.

When we got to the bar where my cousin was working, we had to have a glass of beer first thing, and as I had never tasted beer before, I had a hard time getting it down. My cousin I had only seen once as a small boy, and I had to tell him who I was. Then he took us to a Swedish boarding house and we thought the food was wonderful, as the food on our trip had been so terrible, and besides our money had been low and we could not afford to buy extra food.

Now the next day my cousin took us down to the iron mine and got us all jobs. Three days later we went to work, loading iron ore into wheelbarrows, carting it about one hundred feet to a platform and dumping it into railroad cars. The weather was very hot and the iron ore heavy. Our working hours were ten hours a day at a dollar sixty cents a day. Out of this we paid fifteen dollars a month for room and board.

When evening came I was so tired I could hardly walk uptown, and my hands and feet were blistered. Perhaps my blistered feet were caused by a pair of cowhide boots that I had bought for two dollars. The third day we worked there I was just about ready to give up my job when the foreman from the mine came and spoke Swedish to us. He wanted three men to go down in the mine to work. Right away we threw away our shovels and followed the foreman down to the bottom of the mine, about four hundred and fifty feet underground. It was as cool as a cellar, and I thought heaven could not be any nearer.

I felt fine that evening and the next day the foreman came and put me to work with another gang of men. I could not understand them but listened carefully for several days, trying to pick up a few words of English. After a few days, I told a Swede in our boarding house that I didn't think I could ever learn to speak the English language as I hadn't been able to learn a thing from the men I worked with. He laughed and said naturally I couldn't learn to speak English from them as they were Polacks and couldn't speak any more English than I could.

For about two weeks I got along fine, but one night when we were shoveling iron ore into the train cars I came terribly close to being killed. About a hundred tons of iron ore slid and came roaring down to the spot where we were working. If one of the men working with us had not seen a little dropping of ore and yelled for the four of us to run into the tunnel, we would not have lived to tell the tale, for a half a minute later the avalanche broke. I might add that hardly a week passed that someone was not killed in one of the two mines.

For three months I worked there until the mine closed down. There was not much other work around but I finally landed a job

from a contractor who was making charcoal for the mining company. I worked for him for three weeks at a dollar and a half a day. He was to report my time to the company who was paying the men. However, he never reported any time for me, for when I went to get my money there was no record of my having worked and the contractor had left town.

Our money was getting low again, so my two Swedish friends and I went down the line to a little town called Norway. We got jobs cutting wood for a dollar a cord but as there was about two feet of snow on the ground, and the small maples were nearly frozen, we could only cut about a cord a day per man. After we had been there a month we gave it up and found we had only seven dollars and fifty cents apiece left after paying room and board.

So we went back to Stambaugh again, hoping to get credit at our boarding house where we were known. After Christmas we went to a logging camp on the Wisconsin side, at the large salary of twenty dollars a month and board. When we got there the foreman showed me my bunk in the corner of the log bunkhouse, which I was to share with a stranger. My partners were fortunate enough to bunk together. It was very cold at that time of year, even to ice being formed on the inner wall next to my bed and when I awakened the next morning found my hair frozen fast to the wall. My bed partner I did not see till the following Sunday. He was a teamster and had to care for his horses in the evening, not getting to bed until I had long been asleep, and rising early in the morning to feed them. That he was a teamster I knew without being told, as the odor he left behind smelled strongly of horses. Here we could stand the work all right except that the lice nearly ate us up. Perhaps because I was young and tender I got more than my share. At least I thought so. So we quit and went back to Stambaugh and got cleaned up. After being idle for another month, it seemed like a long time until the mines would open again in

May. So we thought we would try another logging camp but there we had the same trouble and had to quit again and return to Stambaugh to get cleaned up.

We got along all right until the mines opened, for we knew we could get jobs there. They always needed men and greenhorns like us were the only ones they could get. No Americans would work there. We started work again in May and after a few days the foreman and superintendent came and watched me while I was working and I felt sure they were talking about me and afraid that I was to be fired. Soon the foreman called to me in Swedish and told me he had a better job for me. He said the superintendent had asked whose boy I was and when he found out I was alone, said the work was too hard for me and for the foreman to give me the job of pumpman. This job was to watch the steam pumps that kept water out of the mine. I had very little to do and I became lonesome, as I had to be down in the mine all by myself, including Sundays. The job paid a little more, one dollar and seventy cents a day, but I was also paid for Sunday. After being at this job for two months a man from LeHigh, Iowa, arrived in town looking for miners. They had just had a strike and he needed men. He told us that the mine would pay us very well and would also run the year round, so a bunch of us went with him.

Naturally, when we got there we were given the worst spots in the mine to work, as the old-timers had picked off the best places. Our vein was only about two feet thick with not nearly enough room to remove the waste dirt. Consequently, the best two of us could do was dig out about three tons of coal a day at a dollar a ton, making a dollar and a half a day per man for ten hours work. We had only about a three foot space to work in, never could straighten up and had to crawl on our hands and knees to remove the coal to the tramcars. There we could stand up for a few minutes as the tunnel widened to six feet high.

It was very discouraging, for after we had paid sixteen dollars a month for board and bought a few clothes it was almost impossible to save any money. One day I received a letter from a Swedish friend of mine who was in Ouray, Colorado, working in a silver and gold mine. He said he could get me a job there at three dollars and fifty cents a day if I could manage to scrape together fifty dollars for the train fare. At that time I did not have anywhere near fifty dollars and it took me two more months before I had saved sixty dollars for the trip.

So in February of 1889 I decided to go to Colorado as three dollars and fifty cents a day sounded like a great deal of money to us. As these other men were four years older than I and big and strong, I was glad to have them go with me. We bought our tickets as far as Omaha, Nebraska, for seven dollars and fifty cents apiece and then I was supposed to find out in the depot there how much our fare would be to Ouray, Colorado. By that time I had picked up the fair amount of English, so I reported to my partners that the ticket would be thirty-nine dollars and fifty cents. We stood looking at the map on the wall and seeing the name San Francisco printed there, wondered how much money it would take to go there as the distance looked twice as far.

So my friends wanted me to ask the agent how much it would cost to go to San Francisco and he told me thirty-five dollars. We then held a consultation and decided that if we could go twice as far for less amount of money, we might as well go to San Francisco, which we did.

We arrived there the first part of February, just what date I don't remember, but we were there on my birthday, the fifteenth of February, and there was no celebration. Of course we were about broke and stayed in a hotel called the American Exchange for fifty cents a night but had to move on to a cheaper place where we could rent beds for twenty-five cents a night. We walked the streets all day looking for work but no luck.

One evening we stood on a corner on Market Street not far from the waterfront, and all the money we had between us was seventy-five cents. We needed the money for beds but also we were hungry as we had lived on a glass of beer and free lunch for several days. We didn't know whether to spend the money for a bed or get something to eat, so we decided on eating. After our meal we went to the lodging house and told the proprietor that we were broke and couldn't pay for our lodging unless he would loan us ten dollars on two cheap watches of ours. He said he would if we would promise to redeem them.

Now after a few more days hunting, we finally got jobs through an employment office, having to pay out a dollar and a half apiece. We were to report early the next morning at a rolling mill that belonged to the Union Iron Works and we were there long before seven a.m. There I suffered another set-back, for when the boss looked us over he said he could use the others but, looking at me, could not use any school boys. I said I could work as hard as the others but he didn't believe me and wouldn't even let me try. I had to go back to town heartbroken and returned to the employment

agency to see if I could get a refund on my money. The man did not want to give me my money back, but said he would have another job for me the next morning, and it all turned out for the best.

I got a bed to sleep in at the same place on credit but no breakfast the next morning. I returned to the employment agent and he took me up to an architect's office. The architect wanted somebody to take care of his horse and buggy, milk a cow and take care of his yard. He asked me particularly if I could milk and I said "yes" to everything he asked me, I wanted the job so badly. For this I was to receive fifteen dollars a month and room and board. It was the room and board I was most interested in.

Mr. Haven, the man I was to work for, gave me the address at Twenty-fourth and Howard Street. I was to take the street car out but didn't have the courage to ask him for the carfare. I started out and after I had walked a ways started digging in my pockets to see if I had overlooked a nickel, but no luck. However, I found four pennies in my purse. They didn't seem to use any pennies in San Francisco in those days so I didn't even have a chance to spend them. Anyway I got on the small horse-drawn car, put my four pennies in the glass box and as the driver said nothing, I went and sat down.

I got out to the house and reported to Mrs. Haven and she took me out to the barn and showed me the room overhead where I was to sleep. About five o'clock Mr. Haven came home with the horse and buggy and I fed the horse and brushed him. Then the

hired girl called me to come into the kitchen for dinner. She did not have to ask me twice as I'd had nothing to eat that day, not even a free lunch. That was the best meal I have ever had.

Milking the cow worried me as I had never milked before. I asked the hired girl where the cow was as I had not seen any around that day, and she said the cow was in the country. She was about to have a calf and they didn't want her in the barn at the time. Needless to say I was happy and relieved.

The next morning I was to have the horse harnessed at eight o'clock. I got up at six o'clock so I would have plenty of time to feed him and harness him, but when I brought out the harness I was stuck for I'd never seen that type of harness in the old country. When Mr. Haven came out he had to help me do the harnessing and asked me when I had ever taken care of horses. I told him in the old country and he just smiled. Also I hadn't brushed the horse well enough and had to do it over again. The next morning I brushed that horse for an hour but Mr. Haven still found some hairs that did not lie straight on the horse's legs. But from then on I got along fine and liked the people I worked for.

During the day I worked in the yard and didn't have to work too hard. Here I would like to mention that about thirty years later, when Mother and I went to San Francisco, we drove past this same house, and I told her that in the kitchen of that house I had the best meal I had ever tasted in my life. Then I explained to her how I had been so hungry and the circumstances of that story.

After I had worked for Mr. Haven for about two weeks, one of my friends came to see me. He had been fired and was broke. I went to Mr. Haven and asked him for five dollars to give to my friend so he could eat. About two weeks later I was sent to the grocery store to do an errand and when I returned the cow was standing in the barn. As it was early afternoon I thought it would be a good time for me to practice milking. I milked and I milked but not a drop did I get. Then I knew I would be fired as I had told Mr. Haven I could milk a cow.

When the hired girl called me in for dinner I noticed that she was smiling to herself and she said to me, "Those people we are working for are very foolish people." I said I thought they were very nice people. Then she explained to me that they had sent the cow out to a farm to have her calf and she had never had one and consequently dried up. Of course that was the reason I couldn't get any milk and didn't know it. Mr. Haven sold the cow and didn't replace it with any other and my job was saved again. I was very lucky.

Well, after I had been there two months I had saved twenty-five dollars, plus the five dollars loaned to my friend. During that time I had not left the house, so had saved every nickel. At that time my other partner came to see me. He had quit his job at the rolling mill and wanted me to go with him to Point Arena, Mendocino County.

We left, taking a boat up about a hundred miles north of San Francisco to Point Arena. There we got a job right away loading railroad ties at thirty dollars a month, room and board, and a cabin of our own. The work was not too hard, even though we were on the job ten hours a day. That spring I received a letter from my mother saying that she had remarried, which did not surprise me too much. As I explained before, I had always thought that was in her mind when she let me leave home with so little objection.

I had been corresponding with my cousin, Alfred Berlin, who had finally located in Tacoma, and we decided to quit our jobs and go north and see him. I might mention that at that time we had been reading accounts of the Seattle fire in our local newspaper. We left on a boat from San Francisco which took us to Seattle. We had all day to sight-see as our Tacoma boat did not leave till later in the evening.

The business section at that time was on first and Second Avenues, between Yesler Way and Madison Street, and it was all in ashes. This was about a month after the fire and by that time some digging for foundations had started. I remember walking up Second Avenue to Pike Street and saying, "We may as well turn back, we have seen the whole town." Actually Pike Street was graded as far east as Eighth Avenue, but it looked like a county road with a few one-story frame buildings between Second and Fourth Avenues and a few residences beyond there.

That evening we got on the boat again and went to Tacoma and got a room in a lodging house. The next morning we went to look for my cousin, Alfred Berlin. He was boarding with a Swedish family uptown and they told us he was working for the St. Paul & Tacoma Lumber Company. That mill had just been built a year before. We went down to see him. He was working on the log boom, and he knew me right away. We talked to him where he was standing on the logs and he wanted us to meet him that evening uptown in a certain saloon. Then he asked us if we had any money and we said we had lots of money, which was not very much. He pulled out a buckskin sack from his back pocket in his overalls and shook it at us and said, "You don't think I am broke." He had four twenty-dollar gold pieces in the sack, but the buckskin sack had rotted from the salt water and when he shook it at

us two of the twenties went through the sack and into the bay in about twenty feet of water, and I am sure they are still there. But we still had a little celebration that evening. The next morning my partner and I started to look for a job. We got a job to go to work in a brickyard across the bay, about twenty miles from Tacoma. Where it was, I can't tell now, but that was a hard job wheeling brick all day. We had a very poor shack to sleep in and poor food, so we only stayed there three days, got our pay and went back to Tacoma to look for something better.

We got a job to go up to North Bay to a logging camp at thirty-five dollars a month and our board. As was customary in those days in the West, we had to furnish our own blankets, but we liked that better. I had been there only a few days when I got a job that paid me forty-five dollars a month. I worked there that winter and in the spring got a letter from my sister in Sweden. She was then sixteen years old. She did not like to stay home after our mother had married as she did not like her stepfather, and she was coming in July. I went to Tacoma to meet her, but as I did not know what day she was coming I had to meet all trains and boats that came from Vancouver, B.C. Some of the immigrants were sent on the Canadian Pacific Railway and after about a week's time she came on a boat from Vancouver. I got her in with a Swedish family by the name of Benson. Mrs. Benson was very kind to her and helped to get her some clothes. We found her a place to work in an American family at ten dollars a month. As she could not speak a word of English, it was not so easy for the lady to get along with her, so I promised to come and see her the next day. When I came the lady told me I would have to take her away as she could not get along with her. In the meantime, she had told the lady next door that she would have to let her go and when she saw me she came over and wanted my sister to go to work for her. We just moved my sister's little suitcase over to the next house. After a few days the lady told me she would get along with her fine and I could go back to my job. I did not see my sister again until next Christmas. By that time she could talk and understand English a little and she was getting along fine. She worked for the same people for about a year in Tacoma and then they moved to Seattle and she went with them and worked for them about a year in Seattle.

Now the logging camp I had been working in for about a year and a half shut down and I was out of a job again, but had saved up a little money. About this time they laid out the townsite of Fairhaven, which is now South Bellingham, and I got a job to go up there to work for a contractor who was clearing the land and grading the streets. I got a job with the powder man to help him dig the holes under the stumps and the powder man was to put in the dynamite and blast them out of the ground. One day the foreman came to us and wanted us to blast out a stump that stood too close to the edge of the street. He wanted us to put in just a little powder and loosen the stump so they could pull it out. As the roots of the stump went under a nearby shack about 12 by 12 feet in size, which was used to store tools and powder, he did not want us to put much powder under the stump. I don't know how much powder the man put under the stump, but when the blast went off the stump and the house went in the air, and the shovels and tools were scattered all over the townsite. The roof was the only thing that held together but it went in the air and landed about two hundred feet from where the house stood. The powder man got fired and the foreman acted kind of mean to me the rest of the day, so I quit that day and went back to Tacoma.

Then it was hard for me to find another job, so another young fellow and I decided we would take a boat and go back to San Francisco, and from there back to the Redwood country where we had been before. This was in January, 1891.

In 1891 and 1892 I worked in the Redwoods in California, felling timber, and received the large wage of fifty-five dollars a month with room and board. Then in 1893 the Cleveland hard times were being felt and our wages were cut to forty-five dollars a

Redwoods in Mendocino County, California

month, so I decided to quit and go back to Seattle. On arriving there I found most of the logging camps shut down and it was impossible to find a job of any kind. This decided me to move on to Olympia and try my luck. Things were not much better there, and while waiting for some camps to open I took a job on a small freight boat running between Olympia and Shelton. This job entailed loading and unloading freight, which I did for three and a half days, never once removing my clothes and catching only two hours sleep at a time while the boat was running back and forth between the two towns. I decided to quit, and when I went to get my pay it was three dollars and fifty cents in all, and not a nickel for overtime. This led to my getting a short job in Shelton and then on to a job at Mud Bay, Olympia, felling timber for forty dollars a month. Needless to say, I was sorry I left the Redwood country. That summer I worked so hard that I finally had to quit, taking the five hundred dollars I had saved and heading again for Seattle.

All that winter I stayed in Seattle, rooming with a family who lived on Fifth and Pike. This room I shared with another man, and for the two of us our room was one dollar and a half a week.

From there, in the spring of 1894 I went to Arlington, Washington, and got a job with a man who had a little sawmill right in Arlington, and we logged right on the townsite of Arlington. There were only six men and our procedure was to work in the woods three days, haul the logs we had cut to the sawmill, then work for three days sawing the logs into lumber. For this we were paid thirty dollars per month, room and board.

At this rate I was not getting ahead very fast, but continued to work in different logging camps until the summer of 1896, when I went again to Seattle, as I liked it there. My work there was in a Fremont sawmill at a dollar and a half a day, but I was sliding backwards fast, for at the end of three weeks I had spent more than I had made.

About that time I ran across a friend of mine, Peter Henning, who now lives in Stanwood. He had bought some timber on Hood Canal and wanted me to go to work for him, which I did. That was a sad summer for me. One day I was working with another friend, Mr. Johnson, out in the woods cutting trees on a steep side hill. We felled a tree and it started to slide down the hill. On hearing a cry, I turned around and saw the tree carrying my friend with it down the hill. By the time I reached him he was nearly gone and I realized his back was broken. He lived only a few minutes.

We carried him back to camp where we made a rough box out of split cedar boards to carry him in. He was to be buried in Seattle and the problem of getting him there was something. We rowed down the canal sixteen miles, where we found a farmer we could hire to haul the corpse to Silverdale, about four miles away. At that point, we caught a boat and took Mr. Johnson to Seattle for his funeral. I then went back to camp to work, but was so depressed I finally had to leave.

My next thought was to try and be a farmer, so I headed for Arlington, where I bought twenty acres of bottom land about a mile outside of town. That was a hard winter, for I spent my time building a little two-room shack and clearing my land. By spring I had cleared about an acre, which I planted in potatoes. About that time I had decided that I couldn't make a living off of my farm alone, so I went to work for a nearby logging camp, planning to work the summer there and improve my farm during the winter months.

However in August of that summer, I went into Arlington one Saturday night to attend the Odd Fellow Lodge, planning to come back the following morning. Sunday morning I got up and bought a morning Seattle *Post-Intelligencer* paper to read during breakfast. Splashed across the page was the news that "G O L D" had been found in the Klondike in Alaska. A friend and I were sitting there discussing this big news, reading the paper over and over again. Finally I slammed the paper down on the table and said, "I'm going to Alaska; will you go with me?" He thought a minute and said, "No." Then I returned to camp, got my things and what little money I had and by four o'clock that afternoon I was on the train bound for Seattle and a new adventure.

The next morning I was down on the waterfront bright and early to buy my ticket for Alaska, but found there was already a long line waiting for just the same thing. While I was standing in line someone came up and slapped me on the back. It turned out to be an old friend of mine, a Colorado prospector by the name of Segalson. He asked me if I had a partner. I said I had a partner from Arlington, a Mr. Kernahan, whom he knew well. I asked if he would join the two of us and he willingly agreed, then we walked up town together to plan for the trip.

The boat we got passage on was a coal freighter, originally used between Seattle and San Francisco, however it would not be ready for another week. This gave us plenty of time to gather together our gear. We had been warned that we must take everything with us, such as food, tools, heavy clothing and blankets for the bitter winter ahead, and that we could not plan on buying anything in Dawson.

The steamship company was selling first- and second-class tickets on this boat. A reporter from the *Post-Intelligencer* boarded the ship not long before it was to sail and inquired what the difference was between first- and second-class passage. He was told that as far as anyone could see, the only difference was that the first-class passengers slept with the horses and the second-class passengers slept with the mules. Since we had second-class passage, we slept with the mules.

Steamer Willamette, a coal carrier, that I left Seattle on in 1897, bound for the Klondike

We boarded the ship on a Monday morning, one week after we had purchased our tickets, our three horses were also loaded on deck. We then learned that the boat was terribly overloaded, carrying twelve hundred men, six hundred horses and six hundred mules. Old timers later claimed that trip was the largest boatload ever to set sail for Alaska. However, everything went well. We took the Inland Passage and the weather was good for all four days, when we entered the bay where Skagway is now located.

As there was no wharf we had a hard time unloading. Men and equipment were unloaded on a scow and horses and mules, tagged with the owner's name, were dumped overboard and made to swim ashore. We men were, by that time, all ashore and caught and claimed our horses as they came up onto the beach. The next move was to make camp for the night on the beach, and after all the little white tents were pitched it looked like some large army encampment. We were then camped on the present townsite of Skagway.

The next day we started out on the trail, only to find it in very bad shape, having been built that same year in a great hurry. We made only ten miles that first day and back. In this manner, we had to make ten trips to get our outfit up the mountain trail ten miles. After thirty days we had all of our outfit thirty miles up the trail, and had ten miles more to go to Lake Bennett, where we were going to build a boat to carry us to Dawson. From Lake Bennett to Dawson it meant a journey of some six hundred miles across a string of lakes and down the Yukon River.

Up until this time, we had gotten along fairly well. The horses had been loaded with two hundred pounds and each of us had carried a fifty-pound sack of flour on his back. I might add that fifty-pound sack got mighty heavy come evening time. We decided now to change our plan and send two of the men on to Lake Bennett to start construction of the boat we would need. We were all pretty concerned as to whether the horses could stand the trip, as we had only oats to feed them. However, the two other men started off for the Lake and Mr. Kernahan and I went back to the tent to finish packing for the last ten miles. Much to our horror someone had stolen all the feed for the horses and we had nothing left to give them. We decided that I must trek back to Skagway and buy two more horses and more feed. We had heard that lots of men were quitting and putting their horses and equipment up for sale.

I started out the next morning for Skagway, but met an obstacle immediately. I had to cross a mountain creek about ten feet wide and as I had no rubber boots and only a cheap pair of shoes I would get soaking wet before I had even started. Mr. Kernahan suggested putting on his rubber boots and carrying me across on his back, which he did. However, we got half way across the stream and my

White Pass in the winter of 1897-1898

partner slipped when he stepped on a rock, dumping us both in the icy mountain water. I waded over to the other side and sat down to wring out my socks, pretty mad that I was going to have to strike out soaking wet on a thirty-mile hike.

I made Skagway that evening and sat down to fry my bacon and eat my bread. It had snowed and rained all day and I was pretty wet, so I struck out to find a dry place to sleep. In the three weeks we had been gone several rough houses had been built and on one of these was a sign, "Lodging." I went in to inquire about a bunk but found that each bunk had for bedding a pillow and one blanket, and the owner said he couldn't spare any more blankets. Being soaking wet, I knew that was no place for me, so I went out to find another place and came across a large haystack of baled hay covered with canvas. So I said to myself, "me for that haystack." I climbed up under the canvas and opened up two of the bales and crawled in under the hay. Being very tired I slept well all night and by morning my clothes had dried on me. My big mistake was in taking off my shoes the night before and putting them outside, alongside the haystack, for by the next morning my shoes were so frozen I couldn't get them on. I tried to warm them up with my hands but that was slow business. Looking around I saw a blacksmith and I asked him if I could thaw my shoes out over his fire and he said "yes."

The White Pass Trail in the fall of 1897

After that, I looked around for something to eat and found a sign, "Restaurant," on one of the shacks. My breakfast that morning was ham and eggs, and did it taste good! By that time, I was beginning to feel wonderful and started looking around for horses to buy. I found two horses very quickly and bought them, but failed to examine them very carefully. I led them over to a place where oats were sold and then noticed that they had ugly cuts on their hind legs. Of course, I couldn't take them out on the trail, so I went back to the man to return them, but he wouldn't take them back. As I had paid one hundred and twenty dollars for them, I couldn't afford to buy any more. I told the man that if he would return me one hundred dollars and take the horses, I would take a loss of twenty dollars for my foolishness. That was agreeable with him and I was very careful when I bought the next two horses to see that they were good.

By twelve o'clock that same day I started up the mountain with each horse loaded with two hundred pounds of oats. I made ten miles that day and by evening it was pouring rain so I stopped, built a camp fire and cooked myself some dinner. That night I didn't get a wink of sleep as I had to keep my fire going to keep warm. In the morning I repacked the horses and started up the mountain again.

That day it snowed and rained all day and in two places where it was dangerous footing I had to unpack the horses and carry the hundred-pound sacks of oats over the area and come back and lead the horses across. In these two spots on the side of Bare Mountain a great many horses had been lost, falling hundreds of feet down the mountain, and I could not afford the loss of horses or oats.

That evening I stopped at a camp where several men had pitched their tents and asked if I could sleep in with them. They said, "yes," but didn't have any blankets they could loan me, only an old wet canvas that I could roll myself in, if that would help me any. I accepted and rolled up in the damp canvas, but that night was worse than the night before in front of my campfire. I was so cold and wet and spent another sleepless night. When day broke, I crawled out and thanked them, loaded my horses and by noon that day I had reached the summit of the mountain. On the other side it was easier travelling and I made our camp by that night. My partner had been rather expecting me all day and had cooked up a big pot of beans and a large pot of coffee. Nothing ever had tasted so good to me, and with a good night's sleep I felt fine the next day, and we were happy as things seemed to be turning out well again. While I had been gone two of our horses had died from lack of feed but one was still well, so we had three good horses.

We packed the next day and pushed on to Lake Bennett, where

we met our other two partners. We all worked hard and had the boat built by the first of October. It was a job, for we had to cut our own trees and whipsaw our own lumber. The boat, when finished, was capable of carrying all four of us, and four tons of provisions. We were all ready to start when a cold north wind blew up snow and we had to wait three days before the wind changed. We had also butchered our horses, having no further use for them, and saved the hind quarters for eating. As we hadn't had any fresh meat since Skagway, those horse steaks tasted pretty good. Having turned very cold, the meat froze and we knew it would keep.

On the third day of the storm the wind changed, and we hurriedly loaded the boat and shoved off. By evening we had made ten miles and came on a small island where we camped for the night. The boat was leaking a little, so we had to unload it and caulk it. We then pitched our tent and cooked our food, happy that we were again on our way. But the next morning was a different story, for the wind had changed to the north and we woke to find six inches of snow on top of our blankets. We had forgotten to stake down the tent at the bottom the night before. It was quite a job cleaning all the snow out of the tent and getting the cook stove set up inside to make our breakfast. It stormed all day till the following morning, when the weather cleared and we were able to reload the boat and be on our way. That day we made about twenty miles and landed where the Canadian customs officers were stationed, although by that time we had already travelled about fifty miles on Canadian territory.

They were pretty tough on us and even made us pay duty on the rubber boots we had on our feet, which made us pretty mad. Their reason was that we had worn our boots for a good long while on Canadian soil, so there was nothing to do but pay.

From there, we crossed a few more lakes and came into the Yukon River, which took us to the White Horse Rapids. These rapids we had heard were very swift and very dangerous and many boats had been smashed or overturned while trying to get through. As our boat was very heavily loaded, our intention was to unload part of our gear and pack it by land past the rapids while the boat was steered through the rapids by three of our men. However, just at that time we saw several boats go through successfully and decided to try our luck. Mr. Kernahan was put ashore and he stationed himself way below us at the foot of the rapids, where we could throw him a line to pull us ashore. We made it all right and Mr. Kernahan caught our rope and pulled us ashore, where we camped for the night. Incidentally, our boat was still leaking and we had to unload it completely every evening.

By this time the weather was turning colder, with about six inches of snow on the ground. Our method of sleeping was to pitch our tent, cut branches and lay them on top of the snow inside the tent and then lay our blankets on top of the branches. Mr. Segalson was the best cook, so while he did our cooking we did the unloading and pitching the tent.

It was getting so cold by this time that we were afraid the river would freeze before we reached Dawson, so we pushed on as fast as possible, knowing we had no time to spare. As we rowed along in our boat, large chunks of ice floated past us all day. We were finally able to reach the south side of the Klondike River which,

Boats starting for the Klondike in the fall of 1897
(our boat was similar to these)

at this time, had frozen over solid, allowing us to walk over the ice into the town of Dawson. This little town, at that time, was only a year old and as lively a little place as you'd ever see. There were many saloons, dance halls and gambling houses, all waiting for the poor miner to spend his hard-earned gold.

On looking around town for a place to stay, we couldn't even find a room for rent, so the only solution was to build us a cabin. So we picked a spot on the Louse Town side, about half a mile up the Klondike River. It took us about a week to build this cabin and as there was no lumber to be found, we knocked our boat apart and used this lumber for the floors and the door. On each side we left a place to put a window pane, but on looking around for glass found there was none to be had in Dawson. Our next best solution was to use clear whiskey bottles, standing them alongside each other, about ten for each window. This filled up the holes and let in a little light in the day time.

We now divided our outfit into four parts, which gave us only ten candles apiece, to last us the whole winter. We started saving our bacon grease and poured it into a lid of a tin can, with a twist of rag down the middle for a wick. That way we were able to conserve on our precious candles. Just after we had finished building our cabin, we heard of a creek that had not been staked fifty miles from Dawson, and all hurried up there to stake our claims. As most of the creeks around there had been paying heavily in gold dust, we were sure we had struck it rich and wouldn't have sold for $50,000. The name of this creek was All Gold Creek, and very badly named, I must say. I worked that creek for three months until my money ran out and found nothing. I had to look for a job to keep me going.

The first job I got was to help some friends whipsaw some lumber which they needed for sluice boxes. These boxes were used to sluice the dirt taken from the creek bottoms. It was so cold that my toes became frozen and I did not realize it until I came in that evening. The pain that night was terrific and as I worked out again the next day they were no better. Although my toenails all dropped off because of the freezing, they all grew back and I didn't seem any worse for wear. This job only lasted four days so I had to find something else. I found some fellows who had a claim about eight miles up the creek and worked for about a month at fifteen dollars a day.

I felt better with some money in my pocket and looked around for something else to do. I ran across a Mr. Smith who asked me to join him in working his claim and for so doing I could have half of all we took in. After working with him for two months we had found nothing and I had to find another job. Farther up the creek I got a job with another outfit and did well with them, for in four and a half months I had earned eighteen hundred dollars.

I then went on to prospect my own claim, but after three months I gave up as I found no gold. After that I met a man who had a claim on Gold Run, about sixty miles from Dawson, and he wanted to sell his claim to me for three thousand dollars. By this time my eighteen hundred dollars had shrunk to fourteen hundred dollars, and although I thought the claim was a good buy as gold had already been found in this creek, I still didn't have enough to swing the deal. I got in touch with two friends in Dawson and talked them into buying half of the claim. They put up fifteen hundred dollars and I put up my fourteen hundred and threw in my dog that I had bought for one hundred dollars. The difficulty was that my friends who had bought the other half of the claim were in business in Dawson, and it was up to me to do the prospecting and find out if there was any gold. Another friend of mine loaned me his dog and in a few days I struck out for my claim with a sleigh full of provisions, blankets and tools.

I made the sixty miles in three days of hard travelling and the evening I reached our claim it was very cold. On the property was a cabin without doors, windows or floors, so I set up my sheet

iron stove, hung canvas over the openings, cooked myself some dinner and went to bed. The next day I started to sink a shaft, but as the ground was frozen I had to build a fire to thaw it out so I could break the ground. It took me ten days to dig down the twenty feet to bedrock. When I reached the bedrock I found a few spots of gold color, which was encouraging, so I decided to go back to Dawson and get three of my friends who were not working to come and help me. They decided to come and work for me on the chance that I could pay them in the spring when we could wash out the gold, if we found any.

We set to work and sank three more shafts and found a little gold, but there was so little and it was so uneven I was afraid there would not be enough to make it worth while. However, we plugged along, hoping for the best. After working for a month on this claim, I was told that some people had restaked my claim and I had a lawsuit on my hands. This meant that I had to go to Dawson, hire a lawyer and appear before the Canadian Gold Commission. It seems that the party who had restaked my claim had found out that the man I had bought from had not staked the claim himself, but had gotten friends of his to do it for him, which was unlawful. But as they did not have very good evidence, I won the lawsuit and went back to work my claim, a very happy young man.

However, three weeks later I received another summons to appear in Dawson for another lawsuit. It seems that the man who had restaked my claim before had found other witnesses to prove that the original owner had not staked the claim himself. By that time I had found out that the man who was suing me was a government man and a probable friend of the Gold Commissioner. In the meanwhile, the men who owned the claim next to mine had struck the main paystreak and plenty of gold, but no one around knew about this, including myself. Knowing I was in trouble, these men came to me and offered thirty thousand dollars for my claim if I won the lawsuit. One of these men was Dr. Wills, a brother of a banker in Dawson and a school chum of the Gold Commissioner. Because of the connections of Dr. Wills, I was advised that the only way for me to win the case was to agree to their offer. I contacted my silent partners in Dawson and they said that whatever I decided to do was all right with them. Finally I made up my mind to sell, with the result that I won the lawsuit. I feel certain that I would not have won the lawsuit if Mr. Shute and Dr. Wills had not been on friendly terms with the Gold Commissioner.

Some years later I heard that this claim I sold turned out to be very rich, and that Mr. Shute and Dr. Wills cleared over two million dollars from it in two years time. Also they owned the claim next to this one and from the two claims they must have netted around five million dollars before they sold out to a dredging company. I understand that Dr. Wills left Alaska with all of his money and returned to his home in Eastern Canada, but that Mr. Shute stayed in Alaska and soon spent his fortune on poor mining ventures, gambling and drinking. The Yukon Pioneers in Dawson had to keep him until he died.

After I had paid my expenses for the lawsuit and paid off the men working for me, I had about thirteen thousand dollars, which was my share in the claim. This looked like a lot of money to me, so I decided that I had had enough of Alaska and returned to Seattle. My trip home was a lot different than the trip north. In the two years I had spent in the Klondike a railroad had been built

Skagway in the spring of 1898

over the White Pass from Lake Bennett to Skagway, a distance of about forty miles. Going north this part of the trip had taken us forty-three days. On my return, I rode in comfort and the trip was completed in three hours going over the same route. In Skagway I took a passenger boat and completed my trip home in style.

In Seattle I looked up my sister, Mrs. Landstrom. She had been married while I was away to a man who had a job on a boat going from Seattle to Alaska. As she was alone so much of the time, she asked me to spend the winter at her house. When I arrived at her home and she asked where I had my luggage, I had to confess that I didn't have any. I had left my old rags in Dawson. I was in perfect health, which I had had all the time I was away. I hadn't even had a cold while in Alaska, but I was certainly happy to be back and at my sister's house. I had my first bath in over two years. The next day I bought some clothes and took a trip to Arlington to visit some of my friends and see the farm I had started to clear. The farm did not look very good, so I traded it for a house in Arlington which I later sold for five hundred dollars.

Back in Seattle again, I decided to go to business college, more for something to do than anything else, as I had not made up my mind what I wanted to do. Also I bought a lot on Bellevue Avenue between Pike and Pine Streets for eight hundred dollars and had two seven-room houses built on this lot. The two houses together cost only twenty-five hundred dollars, which sounds unbelievable today. After completing the houses, I bought a ten-acre tract of land in Rainier Valley on Juneau Street and Empire Way. During this time, I had renewed my acquaintance with a girl I had taken out a few times before going to Alaska. The next spring this girl, Hilda Carlson, and I were married. This was in May 1900. We took a trip to Sweden for our honeymoon and visited her home and mine. Although we met in Seattle, we were both from the same part of Sweden, our homes being only twenty-four miles apart.

And now I must mention a little history about Mother. She lost her father when she was one year old. Her mother was left with six children and a small farm. As the children grew up, the two oldest ones left for America and finally settled in Seattle. When Mother was fifteen years old she had to go out to work to earn her own living, and so did her other sisters, too, as her mother turned over the farm to her only son then at home, with the agreement that he should keep her the rest of her life. In 1894 the mother and her two daughters decided to come to America and to Seattle where they had a married sister and a brother living in Woodinville. At that time a young man, a cousin of theirs, came back to Sweden from America and was going back again to Colorado. They decided to go with him as he could speak English and they could be with him to New York. After buying their tickets they did not have much money, and turned twenty dollars over to him to keep for them until they got to New York. When they reached Castle Garden in New York where they parted, they took different trains and did not have a chance to get their twenty dollars from him. They were sent over the Canadian Pacific Railway and it took them eight days to get to Seattle. As they had only two or three dollars between them they had to live on that all the way to Seattle, and they had only bread and water for the whole eight days. They had fifteen cents between them when they came to Seattle. Mother at this time was close to eighteen years old, and as they had a married sister here to come to they got along fine. The two sisters went to work and the mother stayed with her daughter and son. I met her at her sister's home, as I had met her sister before.

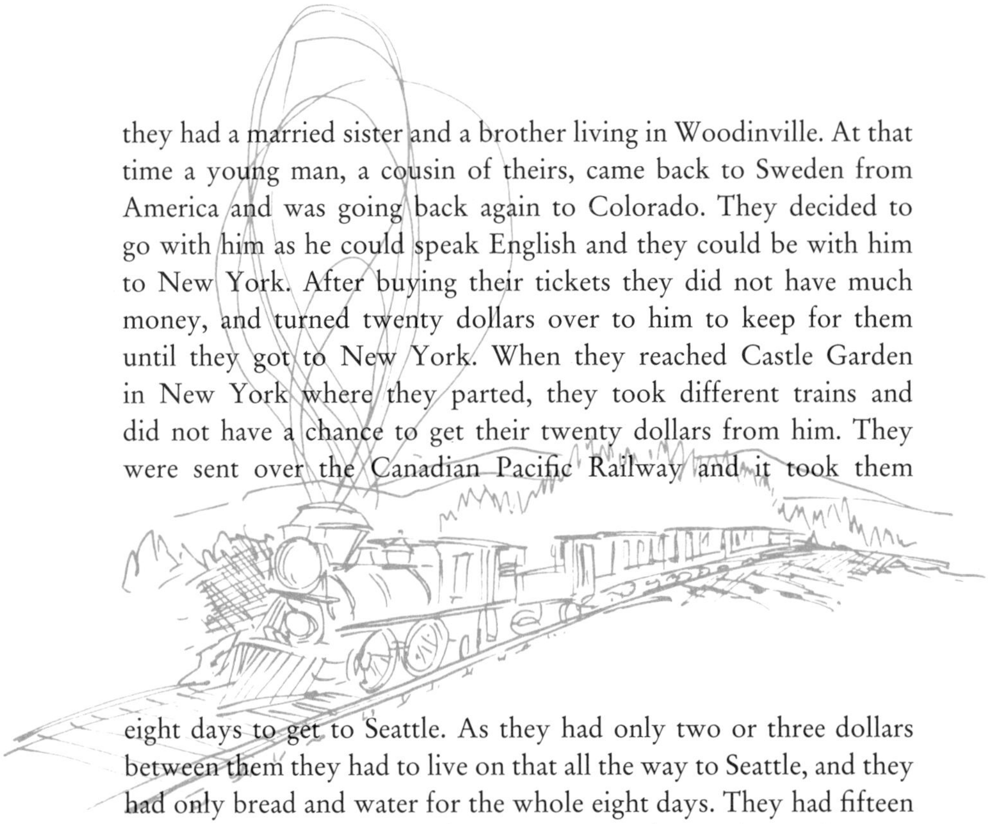

On our return to Seattle in the fall, we moved into one of the houses I had built on Bellevue Avenue. I was still not certain what I wanted to do, and for lack of anything better I started to improve the land in Rainier Valley. After working on it a few months I was quite sure I couldn't make a living from this land and started looking around for some small business to get into.

I had met Mr. Carl F. Wallin in Alaska. He and I left Skagway for the Klondike at the same time, but when we arrived at the first junction he and his partner decided to try the Chilcoot Pass to Lake Bennett and we preferred the White Pass. As it turned out, the Chilcoot Pass, although ten miles shorter, was much more rugged, and Mr. Wallin had to return to Skagway after being on the trail for two weeks. Mr. Wallin was a shoemaker by trade and on his return to Seattle had set up a shoe repair shop on Fourth Avenue and Pike Street, where the Bigelow Building now stands.

I often visited Mr. Wallin in his shop and one day he suggested that we join in partnership and open a shoe store. Mr. Wallin's shop had a ten-foot frontage and when we were able to get the real estate man occupying the next ten feet to move out for only two hundred and fifty dollars we decided to form the partnership of Wallin and Nordstrom, as we now had a twenty-foot store.

I was able to put four thousand dollars into the business and Mr. Wallin added one thousand dollars to that figure. From this total of five thousand dollars we spent fifteen hundred dollars fixing up the store and used the remaining thirty-five hundred buying a stock of shoes. We soon found out, however, that this amount didn't buy a very complete stock. On our opening day, our total sales amounted to twelve dollars and fifty cents. I will never forget that first day. I had never fitted a pair of shoes or sold anything in my life, but I was depending on Mr. Wallin's meager knowledge of shoe salesmanship to help me out. Well, this opening day we had not had a customer by noon, so my partner went to lunch. He had not been gone but a few minutes when our first customer, a woman, came in for a pair of shoes she had seen in the window. I was nervous and could not find the style she had picked out in our stock. I was just about ready to give up when I decided to try on the pair from the window, the only pair we had of that style. I'll never know if it was the right size but the customer bought them anyway. The next day was Saturday, and being open from eight o'clock in the morning to twelve at night, we still only took in forty-seven dollars. It didn't look very rosy, but by the end of the first summer we had Saturday sales that totalled as high as one hundred dollars. We both allowed ourselves a salary of seventy-five dollars a month and got along fine on this amount.

I was very fortunate as I owned the two houses on Bellevue Avenue. We lived in one of them and rented the other for twenty-five dollars a month. The Wallins were renting a home but took in roomers who completely paid for their rent. Now, I want to give our wives a lot of credit for the help they gave us by being very saving and not spending any money but for a bare living. In that way we could save a little money and add to our stock of shoes a little each year. It would have been so easy to spend the little we made each year if Mrs. Wallin and Mrs. Nordstrom had not been so careful with money.

Now after four years we felt we were making progress. By this time we had built up our inventory to eighteen thousand dollars, and eleven thousand of that was paid for. Unfortunately, we were ordered out of our location as they were going to tear down the building and build a three-story brick building, which was later torn down and replaced with the present Bigelow Building.

At this time the Berry Brothers had a shoe store on Second Avenue near Pike Street and were in difficulty. When Mr. James Berry heard we were losing our store, he came to us and offered us their store and stock for twenty-one thousand dollars. Of this amount they wanted ten thousand dollars in cash and the remainder to be paid over a six-months period. We wanted very badly to be on Second Avenue, and the Berry Brothers store was considered at that time quite a modern looking place. Finally we were able to obtain a ten thousand dollar loan from the Scandinavian-American Bank, but I had to put up our two houses and the property on Rainier Valley as security in order to swing the deal.

In our best year in the original Pike Street store our sales were approximately forty-seven thousand dollars. In our first year on

Carl F. Wallin and I in front of our first store at Fourth and Pike where Bigelow Building now stands

My Family
(BACK ROW) *Elmer J., John W. (me), Hilda C. (Mother), Esther (Nordstrom) Smith, Everett W.;* (FRONT ROW) *Lloyd W., Mabel.*

Second Avenue we did a business of about eighty thousand dollars and we were very encouraged. However, after this first year we were notified that this building was also to be torn down as MacDougall and Southwick were building a store on this site. They gave us one year to vacate, and during this year we bought out

another shoe store in the Arcade Building on Second Avenue, just south of Union Street. We didn't want to buy another store because it meant borrowing money again, but it was considered a very good location and it was the only way for us to obtain such a desirable spot.

We were quite successful in this store and after eight years were again getting on our feet when Mr. David Whitcomb, the owner of the Arcade Building, came to us and told us we would have to vacate in two months time as Rhodes Department Store wanted to expand and take over our portion of the building. With this short notice, we were forced to buy out a lease on Second Avenue next door to MacDougall and Southwick, for which we paid two thousand dollars. In this store we were more fortunate and remained for twenty-five years.

The last few years Mr. Wallin and I were partners the business seemed to be going backward instead of going ahead, and I was not happy as we did not seem to agree on anything. In 1928, my oldest son, Everett, was travelling for J.P. Smith Shoe Company of Chicago, so I suggested to him that he quit his job and take my place in the store. If he liked it, I would sell out to my three sons, and on that Everett and Elmer agreed. Lloyd was still at the University. In 1929, Mr. Wallin wanted to sell out and that suited us all, and it turned out for the best. I sold to my three sons in 1930. They remodelled the store on Second Avenue, taking on additional space and making a more modern store out of it.

Now, as I am close to 78 years old, I feel when I look back that, outside of losing our dear girl Mabel in 1919, and losing my dear wife in 1943, I have been lucky all my life. I have the rest of my dear family with me. Esther, my oldest daughter, is now married to Lawrence K. Smith and she is so well taken care of, and her nice children. I have my sons with their nice families near me. I have so much to be thankful for, as I could never dream in my young days I would ever live to this age and have things so nice as I now have. It gives me a lot of pleasure to go to the store every day and see the success my sons have made in the business.

In 1946

Mother and I at Hood Canal, 1940

MY AFTERTHOUGHTS

In reading what I have written about my life, I realize that I have made very little mention of the person who has been most responsible for the small success I have had in this country. This person, my wife, made it possible to make progress in the shoe business in the early stages by being so very economical in our home and always encouraging me to go forward when reverses in our business would give me reason to be discouraged. If it had not been for her, I am certain that I would have given up in the first few years of our business as our efforts at that time seemed so futile.

When our business was three years old, in 1904, we built a home on our ten acre tract in Rainier Valley at Juneau Street and Empire Way, and we moved there with the three children who were born by that time. At this place we had a horse and a cow, a few chickens and turkeys. My wife would take care of the chickens and milk the cow and it was my job to look after the horse.

In 1913 we decided to buy a piece of waterfront on Hood Canal to use as a summer place and to be with some of our friends who had purchased tracts adjoining. Here we built two tents and a little kitchen in between, and had many happy days; but actually, it was very rough and it was again pioneering which my wife and I had had enough of by this time, but we used the place every summer regardless for the next thirty years, because we felt it was the best place for our children to spend the summers. Here again, I do not think I would have put up with the discomforts of such a summer place, except that Mother, as I called her, insisted because of the benefits the children were receiving. It was this spirit of Mother's that helped

The Seattle Store, Fifth and Pike (1950)

University District Store

not only me but my family during the years, as she was so inconsiderate of herself and yet so considerate of the welfare of me and our children.

A couple of years later, in 1916, we moved from the country to my present home, which is in Montlake, and which we all liked so very much. Here again the reason for our move was to be handy to the University and a nice district in which to bring up the children.

There are many things that I look back upon my life and experiences with pride, but one of the things that gives me the greatest amount of satisfaction is the progress of our shoe business. When Mr. Wallin and I retired from the business we had a downtown store and one in the University District; and since that time the store downtown and the University store have been enlarged and three other shoe departments have been added; one in Rhodes Department Store in Seattle, another in Lou Johnson's apparel in Tacoma, and a third in Adams, Inc., at Bellingham; and now a lease has been signed for a new store which is being built at Northgate, which is a new section just north of the Seattle city limits, and negotiations are under way for a new store to be built in Portland, Oregon. This growth of the shoe business, which Mr. Wallin and myself started, has given me a lot of satisfaction that our early efforts were justified, but the progress of my dear family has, of course, meant by far the most of all. There is my daughter, Esther, and her husband Lawrence Smith and their children, Marilyn, who this summer became Mrs. Don Gamble, and David and Larry who are now attending the University of Washington. And, there is my son, Everett, and his wife Elizabeth, and their son Bruce, now attending Roosevelt High School, and Anne, who is in the eighth grade at Helen Bush. Also, my son Elmer and his wife Katherine and their sons John and James, who are in grammar school; and my youngest son Lloyd and his wife Illsley and their three daughters, Loyal and Linda, who are in grammar school, and Susan, who has just started her first year of school.

I am so very proud of my children and grandchildren and feel so lucky because of the happiness they have brought me; and also feel that they are lucky for the opportunities afforded them in this grand country.

Our family home since 1916

The Present Store, Fifth and Pike (1962)

MY AFTER, AFTERTHOUGHTS

When I wrote the material for this little book twelve years ago I certainly had no notion that I would still be around in 1962. Also, I had no notion that at this time it would be necessary to order another printing.

My original intention was to jot down memories from my life so that my grandchildren, at a later date, could read something about their Old Country background. Little did I know that I would be here to see eight of my ten grandchildren married and each one with children of their own. I guess I made a mistake. I should have waited until now to write my memoirs, because my life certainly has been fruitful these last twelve years. The trouble is that I find memory doesn't improve with age. At the age of ninety-one I can remember clearly the incidences in my life fifty, sixty, seventy and eighty years ago but don't ask me what happened yesterday. So, the story of the last twelve years must be sketchy but it isn't important because my grandchildren have been living and enjoying this period with me.

For the record only, I want to record the additions to my family since 1950. Granddaughter Marilyn Smith, whom I have noted married Don Gamble in 1950, now has three children, Kim, Larry and Don Jr.

David Smith married Barbara Lofgren and they now have three girls, Karen, Kristen and Kellen. Bruce Nordstrom married Fran Wakeman and they have two boys, Blake and Peter. Anne Nordstrom is now Mrs. Don Hopen and they have a boy, John, and a girl, Susan.

Part of my family taken on my 90th birthday!

(FRONT ROW) *David Smith, Everett Nordstrom, John W. Nordstrom, Jim Nordstrom* (LOWER ROW), *Elmer Nordstrom, Lloyd Nordstrom, Bruce Nordstrom.*

(REAR ROW) *Anne Hopen, Sally Nordstrom, Barbara Smith, Illsley Nordstrom, Kitty Nordstrom, Libby Nordstrom, Linda Mowat, Fran Nordstrom.*

John Nordstrom married Sally Boid and they also have a girl and a boy, Kristin and James.

Loyal Nordstrom is married to John McMillan and their three children are: Keri, John and Lawrie.

James Nordstrom married Sally Anderson and they have one youngster, John Daniel. Linda Nordstrom is now Mrs. David Mowat and they have a girl, Kimberley.

At this point, the unmarrieds are Larry Smith and Susan Nordstrom. Larry is now settled in California in the Bay Area, and Susan will be going East to college this fall.

And the additions have not been confined to my family. It has been a great satisfaction to watch the continual growth of our business. Our main store in Seattle is now considered to be the largest shoe store in America. There are now eight Nordstrom stores in the Pacific Northwest and we are operating thirteen shoe departments in department and specialty stores in the States of Washington, Oregon and California. Another Nordstrom store will be opened in six weeks in Seattle. A lease has been completed for a shoe department in Phoenix, Arizona and a couple of more Nordstrom stores are in the planning stages.

It is hard for me to believe that the little business I started with Mr. Wallin sixty-one years ago could grow to its present size. But, more satisfying is the fact I am here to watch the third generation of our family in the process of taking over the management of this business and doing it so well.

July, 1962

1971

AND NOW IT'S 1971!

Dad passed away in October 1963 just one year after he had ordered another run of this book.

In the 1962 printing he added, "My After, Afterthoughts" which recorded the growth of his family since 1950 and also the growth of the business.

Now in March 1971 we are having a few more books published because many of our friends who worked with Dad or who enjoyed visiting with him in the store have requested copies, and because the family and the business growth is unabated, we take the liberty of using his memoirs as a family record.

Dad's list of great grandchildren has grown to twenty-nine. Since 1962 the Bruce Nordstroms have another son, Erik. The John Nordstroms have a John Elmer Jr. The McMillans have had two additions, Wendy and David Lloyd. The Jim Nordstroms also have two additions, James and Charles. The latest David Mowats are David, Mark Lloyd and Mari. The youngest of the grandchildren, Susan Nordstrom, is now married to Rick Eberhardt and they have three children, Elise, Ricky and Paul. And we just received word that Larry Smith has married Melanie Cahill and they have a son Eric. Larry was the last hold out so now each of Dad's ten grandchildren is married and raising families of their own.

In the summer of 1963 we purchased Best's Apparel, Inc. which at the time included two fine stores specializing in

Women's Apparel. The stores are at Fifth and Pine, Seattle and Lloyd Center, Portland, Oregon. Since then we have merged the two businesses and changed the name to Nordstrom Best, Inc. In 1965 the first combination store of women's apparel and shoes was built in the Northgate Shopping Center, Seattle.

Also in 1966, a fine women's apparel store in downtown Portland, Oregon, Nicholas Ungar, was purchased and later remodeled and joined with our shoe store. The name was changed to Nordstrom Best, and is now one of our most attractive units.

In 1967 a Nordstrom Best store was built in Tacoma Mall and complete menswear and children's clothing departments were added. In 1968 and 1969 stores were built in Bellevue and Southcenter.

Additional leased shoe departments are now being operated in San Antonio, Albuquerque, along with six Liberty House Stores in Hawaii, and three Northern Commercial Co. Stores in Alaska.

A lease for a new enlarged store in Yakima has just been signed. Planned leased shoe departments will open soon in San Jose, Sacramento and Hayward, California.

Plans for an addition to the downtown Seattle store are almost completed and in early fall we expect to begin construction. An artist's sketch of this store is shown along with photographs of the stores competed since 1963.

EVERETT
ELMER
LLOYD

The Lloyd Center Stores, Portland, Oregon (1963)

The Northgate Shopping Center Store, Seattle (1965)

The Downtown Store, Portland, Oregon (1966)

The Tacoma Mall Store (1967)

The Bellevue Store (1968)

The Southcenter Store (1969)

Artist's sketch of the enlarged Downtown Seattle Store (as of 1972-73)